108 Days of God's Kisses

12 KISSES — Keep It Simple Solutions of Self-Care

By Bee Godskiss Daley

Copyright 2015 Bee Godskiss Daley
All rights reserved.
ISBN:0692457003
ISBN 13:9780692457009

No part of this book or any of its contents, including graphic designs, may be reproduced, copied, modified or adapted, without the prior written consent of the author. The graphic designs are protected by U. S. copyright laws and are not to be reproduced, copied, modified or adapted, without obtaining written consent from the author.

DISCLAIMER:

The author of this book does not dispense medical advice or prescribe the use of any technique as a form of treatment for physical, emotional, or medical problems without the advice of a physician either directly or indirectly. The intent of the author is only to offer information of a general nature to help you in your quest for emotional, spiritual, and physical wellbeing. In the event you use any of the information in this book for yourself, which is your constitutional right, the author and the publisher assume no responsibility for your actions.

This is an image I saw one day while I was meditating and it reminded me of the verse in Exodus 3:14, "And God said unto Moses, I AM that I AM" in response to Moses asking God what His name was. Since the original version of this was written so long ago, it is almost impossible to know whether the "AM" was really "AUM," and the translator changed it to "AM" because he did not understand "AUM." What if God was telling Moses that His name was "I AUM that I AUM"? Or what if it was written "I OM that I OM," and the translator changed it to an "A" to "I AM"? In Revelation 22:13, it says "I am the Alpha and the Omega, the First and the Last, the Beginning and the End." It is really interesting that the chemical symbol for Alpha is "A" and the chemical symbol for Omega is written as "Om" and if you put them together, you have "AOm" — another possibility for the name of God which might have been shortened to "AM" because the translator did not understand what this meant? It is fascinating to consider this new definition for the word "OM," isn't it? What if saying "OM" is a way of sending God's kisses out into the world? God created with His words, so this concept of creating and sending out God's kisses with our words or voices is fascinating to me. What if we taught our

children to worship by sending out God's kisses to the world: "I OM that I OM" or just simply "I OM" or "OM"? In many religious traditions, there is a common belief that there is power in the name of the Lord (whatever name you have given the Lord in your tradition). Many yogis will tell you that meditation is the highest form of worship. What if these were the instructions for meditation/worship and we misunderstood or didn't ever figure it out?

Praise the Lord became my mantra over and over again when I had unexpected events happen to me — especially unexpected financial expenses that seemed to come out of nowhere sometimes.

After going to Al-Anon for 23 years and hearing thousands of personal stories, I realized that the one common denominator for 90% of the people there was some type of a financial crisis. The financial crisis was either created by themselves in response to a loved one's addiction or it was indirectly created for them by the loved one's addiction. Better self-care, especially financial, has been the backbone of my recovery and personal transformation. More people talk about their sexual histories when dating than they talk about their money and financial histories. For some reason money is a very taboo subject — even once you are married or in a serious relationship. So, I decided that it was time to gather others to come together to share our experience, strength and hope specifically with the financial challenges that came from addiction and it's effects in our lives. I hope that there are some tools in this book that will help you on your journey to have better financial self-care specifically and generally improved self-care for the rest of your life.

12 KISSES of Self-Care —
Keep It Simple Solutions

1. Listen to your body — if not comfortable, don't do it - especially with money.
2. Be honest — say "exactly" what you mean without being mean. Be honest about your money.
3. Set healthy boundaries and don't be a people pleaser at your own expense.
4. Trust your gut and trust your instincts when making choices. Don't spend when uncomfortable.
5. Practice positive affirmations and never speak bad about yourself. Accept your mistakes.
6. Follow your dreams and never give up on your dreams. "I have all the resources I need."

7. Don't take on too much and don't be afraid to say "No."
8. Be open to trying new things and don't be afraid to say "Yes."
9. Make nurturing choices and be KIND to yourself. Treat yourself once in a while.
10. Accept people, places and things and let go of what you can't control. — Other's financial choices.
11. Pull others into your peace and stay away from drama and negativity. Don't sink with someone else.
12. Raise your vibrations — LOVE.

12 of God's Kisses Money Can't Buy:

1. *Good Manners/Kindness*
2. *Strong Morals*
3. *Respect for self and others*
4. *Good Character*
5. *Quality Relationships*
6. *Basic Common Sense*
7. *Well behaved children/family members*
8. *Trust in self and others*
9. *Patience*
10. *Class*
11. *Integrity in all areas of your life*
12. *LOVE*

This book is dedicated to my fellow spiritual travelers who are looking for "Heaven on Earth" in spite of life's challenges along the way

I wrote this book with inspirational quotes and phrases to use to keep myself focused on my self-care and values every day. I wanted to remind myself that my self-care (especially financial) is essential to my well-being. I hope it helps you to achieve the experience of "Heaven on Earth" in all your affairs.

Day 1
Nothing on earth like God's Kiss — Rumi

Look for God's kisses throughout the day. Pay attention to unexpected "gifts" from the Universe or Spirit today. What was the price for those kisses? Were some of them free? Were some worth it? Were some not worth the price?

Day 2

KISS — Keep it Simple and Serene

How can you simplify something in your life today? Is there something you could do for someone else that would simplify their day today? Can you simplify your money today?

Day 3

*Don't forget to fall in love with yourself first.
Do you love all of you — inside and out? Can you list 5 good things about your body?
Can you list 5 good things about your character? Can you list 5 good things about you that money can't buy?*

Day 4

*You have no need to travel anywhere.
Journey within yourself.
Enter a mine of rubies and bathe in the splendor of your own Light.* —Rumi

What are the rubies within you? Are they priceless?

Day 5

I can heal a broken heart with just a smile — Rumi
Who has a smile that warms your heart? Is there someone you know that would benefit from one of your smiles? What is the price of those heartwarming smiles?

Day 6

Let no one ever come to you without leaving better and happier. Be the living expression of God's kindness; kindness in your face, kindness in your eyes, kindness in your smile, kindness in your warm greeting. — Mother Teresa

Kindness has no price tag

Day 7

Kind words can be short and easy to speak, but their echoes are truly endless. — Mother Teresa

Have you spoken kind words to yourself today? Have you spoken kind words to others today? Have someone's kind words lifted you up when you really needed it?

Day 8

What is your relationship with giving and receiving? Do you give too much away to others and not have enough left for yourself? Do you prevent yourself from receiving kindness/gifts from others because you feel unworthy or undeserving? How can you have more balance between giving and receiving in your life?

Day 9

What does transformation mean to you? When we cook, we transform ingredients into something new — eggs, sugar and flour become cookies. What is something in your life you would like to transform? Do you want to transform your money or the way you spend/use your money?

Day 10

Just when the caterpillar thought the world was over, it turned into a butterfly. Transformation takes time to grow and evolve from one thing to another. Is there something you would like to transform and have become as light as a butterfly in your life? Do you need to be patient to allow the full transformation to take place?

Day 11

The present moment contains past and future. The secret of transformation is in the way we handle this very moment. — Thich Nhat Hanh

Yesterday is a cancelled check, tomorrow is a promissory note and today is cash to spend freely. What is worth your time/energy/cash today?

Day 12

Real transformation requires real honesty. If you want to move forward — get real with yourself!
Bryant MacGill

How honest are you with yourself? Can you be completely honest or do you want to deny or not know what is really going on because of being afraid of the truth of what is going on?

Day 13

FROG — Fully Rely on God (Spirit)

Are you able to fully rely on anyone — someone you can always count on? Can you fully rely on God to provide and take care of all your needs — physical, emotional, mental and spiritual? What are some small things you can do to strengthen your trust?

Day 14

I can do things you cannot, you can do things I cannot; together we can do great things — Mother Teresa

Do you like being part of a team where each person's skills and strengths are a benefit to the entire group? Or do you prefer to work on projects by yourself with only one or two other people helping you with your work?

Day 15
Be.YOU.tiful

Do you completely love and accept your uniqueness as a human being? Do you feel like you are your "authentic" self all the time? What are the obstacles that prevent you from loving your body? Your emotional issues? What prevents you from being "authentic?" One small thing to do today?

Day 16
ROCK This Planet With Love

What would it look like if this entire planet was rocking with Love? Would it be a big party and celebration? Or a quiet, cozy event? Can you take a few minutes to imagine planet Earth rocking with Love?

Day 17

Health is the greatest gift, contentment is the greatest wealth, faithfulness the best relationship. Buddha

What are the greatest gifts in your life (either present or in the past)? Are you content with your financial status? Are you happy with your relationships? What would you like to change?

Day 18
Chakra One (Body); Chakra Four (Mind); Chakra Seven (Spirit) — Body, Mind and Spirit work optimally when they are balanced within us. In physics the balance point is in the middle — Chakra Four (Heart Chakra) - Mind. Where do you feel out of balance in your life? Need more balance?

Day 19

Who you are speaks so loudly I can't hear what you're saying — Ralph Waldo Emerson

What is the message you send to the world when you aren't talking? What is the message you would like to send to the world without speaking? Do your clothes, mannerisms, and expressions match the message?

Day 20

There are no two snowflakes the same and no two fingerprints the same. Over 7 billion unique fingerprints. Do you appreciate your uniqueness? Do you embrace/love your unique "fingerprint" that you were born to share with the world? What do you want your fingerprint to look like on the world's canvas?

Day 21

Love alone can transform insanity, confusion and strife. Love alone can bring about beauty, order and peace. — Krishnamurti

Is there an area of your life where you would like to have more beauty, order and peace? What would that look like? More order in your choices — financial or otherwise?

Day 22
De tout Coeur — Put your heart into it

What do you put your whole heart into? Your work, your relationships, your hobbies, your dreams? Do you spend your money the same way? Do you spend more money on things that you value greatly? What is worth the most money to you? 5 top things to spend on?

Day 23

May he grant your heart's desires. —
Psalm 20:4

What are your heart's desires? Do you want a fabulous collection of shoes? or sports cars? or video games? dvd's? What are all the desires of your heart? Have you ever made a list of all of the things your heart desires? 5 things?

Day 24

He is not the God of the dead, but the God of the living. — Mark 12:27

What does it mean to you to be fully alive? When is a time or times in your life that you have felt most alive and vital? Do you spend your money on things that are nurturing and supportive of making you feel more vital and alive?

Day 25

Every day you have a choice. Choose LOVE. What is your definition of choosing Love? What are choices that are life-giving for you? Is it getting 8 hours of sleep at night? Is it getting a massage? Is it taking an afternoon to go see a movie? Or go visit a museum? Or spend time with a friend?

Day 26

Most folks are about as happy as they make up their minds to be. — Abraham Lincoln

Do you consider yourself a happy person? Do you spend time thinking about things that make you happy? or sad? or your problems? Do you need to spend money to feel happy? What thoughts make you happy?

Day 27

If we have no peace, it is because we have forgotten we belong to each other. Acts of love are acts of peace. — Mother Teresa

What are acts of peace for you? Do you try to keep the peace at your own expense? Is it worth it to you to try to keep peace in your family? in your workplace? in your neighborhood? in your mind?

Day 28

Do not let what you cannot do interfere with what you <u>can</u> do. — Bill Bradley

Do you stay focused on what you want when you are in a difficult situation? Can you make a list of things or think of one or two things you can do today that will help you with your goals? What is something you can do today?

Day 29

When someone loves you, the way they say your name is different. You know that your name is safe in their mouth. — Billy - Age 4

Who do you like to hear saying your name? Are their people that you dread hearing them say your name? Is there someone you love who could benefit from hearing you say their name today?

Day 30

Whatever you do, work at it with all your heart. — Colossians 3:23

Do you try to do your best in all of your endeavors? What prevents you from trying to do your best all the time? Is doing something in a "half-hearted" way acceptable to you? What is one thing that you would like to do your best job?

Day 31

We are carriers of God's Love — Mother Teresa

Have you ever thought of yourself as a carrier of God's Love? What would your actions during the day look like if you were physically carrying around God's Love and delivering it to the people you encounter throughout the day? Who is a carrier of God's love in your life?

Day 32

I will sing a new song unto thee, O God — Psalm 144:9 What is your favorite song? What are the words to that song? Do you have something you tell yourself mentally over and over? Would those words/thoughts make a happy song? sad song? angry song? Do you want to change the words to your song?

Day 33

I will trust and not be afraid: for the Lord Yahweh is my strength and my song.
— Isaiah 12:2

One of the translations for Yahweh is "I Am"

It could be "I OM" as well and OM is considered a universal mantra in the world of yoga. What do you do when you are afraid? Do you pray to God?

Day 34

Acceptance is one of the hardest things — Mother Teresa

Do you have a hard time accepting people, places and things in your life and wish/want to change them to be different somehow? Are you able to completely accept yourself with all of your strengths and weaknesses?

Day 35

Learn how to see. Realize that everything connects to everything else. — Leonardo da Vinci

Have you ever thought about how your money connects you to everyone else? Who do you want to be connected to with your money? Where does most of your money go?

Day 36

Treating yourself like a precious object will make you strong — Julia Cameron

How do you treat precious objects? Do you treat yourself that way? What could you do to treat yourself in a precious way? What kind of pampering or special things would/could you do for yourself?

Day 37

Happiness does not depend on what you have or who you are. It solely relies on what you think. — Buddha

What do you spend most of your time thinking about? Do you think about your work? your problems? your complaints? your joys? Where does your mind go most of the time?

Day 38

One filled with joy preaches without preaching. — Mother Teresa

Do you know someone that is filled with joy? Are you filled with joy? What would it take for you to be filled with joy? Does being kind to yourself make you feel more joyful? What is one thing you could do today that would make you feel joyful?

Day 39

We never repent of having eaten too little. — Thomas Jefferson

Have you ever eaten too much and then regretted making that choice? Are there any activities that you have done too many times and then regretted it? Have you ever spent a lot of money and then regretted it? Are you able to forgive yourself?

Day 40

To keep a lamp burning we have to keep putting oil in it.
— *Mother Teresa*

What is the "oil" that makes you feel alive and vital? What is the minimum you need each day to keep your lamp at least half full with oil? Do you need some quiet time 10 minutes a day? Do you need to exercise on a regular basis? More sleep each night?

Day 41

The tongue has the power of life and death. — Proverbs 18:21

What are the most "life-giving" words you have ever heard? Do you talk to yourself with "life-giving" words and kindness? Are you able to spend your money in "life-giving" ways? for yourself? for others?

Day 42

People only see what they are prepared to see. — Ralph Waldo Emerson

Have you been blind sighted by someone's else's financial choices or mistakes? Were there warning signs ahead of time that you recognize when you look back at the events leading up to the crisis? What did you see that you really didn't want to?

Day 43

Yesterday I was clever, so I wanted to change the world. Today I am wise, so I am changing myself. — Rumi

What is one thing you would like to change about yourself? Would you like to have more willpower in your choices? Would you like to change how much money you have or don't have?

Day 44

Why are you looking for treasure outside yourself when the real treasure house is within you? — Rumi

What do you treasure the most in your life? Your accomplishments? Your job? Your house? Your family? What is your most treasured possession? What is worth the most money to you? What do you treasure about yourself?

Day 45

Love is the dance of your life. Hence those who do not know what love is have missed the very dance of life.
— Osho

Do you feel like you are fully participating in the "dance" of life? What is love worth to you? What is something you can do for yourself to strengthen your love of yourself today?

Day 46
I am wonderfully made —
Psalms 139:14
Do you think of yourself as wonderfully made? Do you think of others as being wonderfully made? What makes them wonderfully made to you? What are your unique skills/qualities that make you wonderfully made? Are you able to set healthy boundaries (including financial) for yourself?

Day 47

Giving power away. Do you let others make financial decisions for you because you think they know better? Do you want to take your power back and start making better financial choices for yourself? What can you do to strengthen your confidence in your ability to manage your financial choices better?

Day 48

People will forget what you said, people will forget what you did, but people will never forget how you made them feel. — Maya Angelou

How do you want other people to feel when they think about you? Do other people think of you as being generous with your money? Or stingy with your money?

Day 49

What are your "money" slogans that you learned growing up? "Money doesn't grow on trees." "Easy come, easy go." "The money is gone, it is ok because I will make some more." "Spend as little as possible." "Spend every dime you have." Do these "slogans" influence your financial choices today?

Day 50

Realize that everything connects to everything else.
— Leonardo daVinci

What connects you to other people, places and things? Does your money connect you to other people, places and things? If you changed the way you spend your money, would some of your connections change?

Day 51

Everything is energy and that is all there is to it. Match the frequency of the reality you want and you cannot help but get that reality. —Albert Einstein

Do you think of yourself as someone with a lot of energy? Or someone with low energy? Do you think of your money as energy? How do you spend most of your money/energy?

Day 52

Who is the most generous person you know? Are they generous with their time, their attention, their money? In what ways are they generous to others/you? Is generosity the same as kindness to you? Are you able to be generous to yourself? Are you able to be kind to yourself? What is something generous/kind to do today?

Day 53

Take delight in the LORD, and he will give you the desires of your heart. — Psalm 37:4

What are the desires of your heart? If you could have anything, absolutely anything you wanted, what would it be? More love? More money? More possessions? More peace in your life? Better health?

Day 54

But as for you, ye thought evil against me; but God meant it unto good. — Genesis 50:20

Has anyone deliberately tried to harm you or hurt you before? Did that experience make you a stronger person? A wiser person? A kinder person? Did you learn a valuable lesson you could not learn any other way?

Day 55

Thy word is a lamp unto my feet, and a light unto my path. — Psalm 119:105

What are the words you use to guide you through your daily life and choices? Do you speak kind words to yourself throughout the day? What are the words you use to guide your financial choices throughout the day? Are these words kind words?

Day 56

What is your favorite possession? Why — what do you like about it that makes it your favorite thing? Where did you get it? Was it a gift or something you purchased yourself? Did it cost you/someone else a lot of money? What are your favorite things that money can't buy for you?

Day 57

Environment is stronger than will. — Paramahansa Yogananda

What is your favorite environment to be in? Does your favorite environment make you feel happy and glad to be alive? Are your financial choices affected by the environment where you spend most of your time? Are these choices nurturing or toxic for you?

Day 58

Be comfortable within your purse. — Paramahansa Yogananda

Are you comfortable with your money? Are you comfortable with the way you spend your money? Are you comfortable with the way money is spent/handled in your family? What would make you more comfortable with your purse?

Day 59

Choose carefully the people you associate with. — Paramahansa Yogananda

How do the people around you affect you? Do you make good choices for yourself with some people and toxic choices for yourself with other people? Would it help you to change some of the people that you associate with?

Day 60

Paradise is within you, in your state of no-mind. And Hell is also within you in your very mind. — Osho

What do you spend most of your time thinking about? Do the things you think about make you feel happy and uplifted — Paradise? Do your thoughts affect the choices you make about the way you spend your money?

Day 61

Say what you mean, mean what you say, but don't say it mean. — Al-Anon

Do you say what you mean when people ask you to do things you don't want to do? Do you use money as a reason to say no instead of telling the truth? Do you say "Yes" with your money when you really wanted to say "No"?

Day 62

Beauty is how you feel on the inside and it reflects in your eyes. — Sophia Lauren

Who is the most beautiful person you know? What makes them beautiful to you? Do you know someone or can you think of someone who has really sparkly eyes? Do their sparkly eyes make them beautiful to you?

Day 63

You are contributing a huge piece of healing here by your willingness to tell the truth over and over again no matter how painful. — Marissa Gottlieb Sarles

What does it cost you to tell the truth? Do you always tell the truth to yourself? Do you tell the truth about what you can/cannot afford to pay?

Day 64

Everything starts with prayer. — Mother Teresa

What does prayer mean to you? Does it cost you anything to pray? Does it take extra time you want to spend on something else? Does it require you to surrender your pride that you can handle everything yourself? Does it require you to surrender to a power greater than yourself?

Day 65

To pray is to allow God to come alive in us. — Mother Teresa

What does it mean to you to have God come alive in you? Would it bring more grace and ease into your life if you allowed God to come alive in you? What would happen to your money and your relationship with your money if you allowed God to come alive in you?

Day 66

As you start to walk on the way, the way appears. — Rumi

Is there a project you have been wanting to start but putting it off because you are not certain of how to go about it so you just don't start at all? Can you start to take some baby steps on this project and see if you find/discover the next step?

Day 67

Why are you looking for treasure outside yourself when the real treasure house is within you? — Rumi

Do you spend a lot of time searching for worldly treasures? Have you spent any time paying attention to and developing the real treasures within you? What are your unique "treasures" that you are here to share with the world?

Day 68

Be not conformed to this world; but be ye transformed by the renewing of your mind. — Romans 12:2

What does it mean to you to renew your mind? Does it mean changing the things you think about? Does it mean changing the way you think about things — including yourself?

Day 69

Let everything that hath breath praise the Lord. — Psalm 150:6

What is something you can praise God for? Is it a beautiful sunrise or sunset? Beautiful trees or flowers or flowing water? What are God's (Nature's) gifts that you are grateful for? Does it cost you anything to be grateful for God's gifts in your life?

Day 70

When you stand and share your story in an empowering way, your story will heal you and your story will heal somebody else. — Iyanla Vanzant

Have you ever shared your story in public? Did it help you feel better after you shared your story? Did it help anyone else feel better? What did it cost you to tell your story?

Day 71

Your task is not to seek love, but merely to seek and find all the barriers within yourself that you have built against it. — Rumi

Do you have a hard time letting yourself receive kindness and love from other people? Do you feel suspicious of the motives of the other person being nice to you for "no reason"?

Day 72

Dwell on the beauty of life.
— Marcus Aurelius

What is beautiful in your life? Do you spend much time thinking about the beautiful people, places and things that are a part of your life? Can you name some of the beautiful people, places and things in your life? What is something beautiful in your life that you can't buy with money?

Day 73

Be your note. — Rumi

Are you able to be your own unique self all the time? If not, what stops you from being true to yourself all the time? Are you afraid of being teased or criticized or misunderstood? Are you able to be your authentic self all the time with your money? What prevents you from being authentic and honest with your money?

Day 74

80% of what we take in is through our eyes — Louis Schwartzberg

What do you take in visually every day? Do you spend time in an environment that is visually nurturing for you? Is there something small you could do that would make your physical environment more visually nurturing for you?

Day 75

What does your daily self-care routine consist of? Does it include time to be kind to yourself— especially with your money? Are you able to set healthy financial boundaries as part of your self-care? Are you able to make sure you have enough money to pay for your necessities before you give/help someone else financially?

Day 76

I have set before you life and death, blessings and curses. Now choose life......Deuteronomy 30:19

What does it mean to you to choose life? Do you make choices that feel good to your body? Have you made choices (including financial choices) before that didn't feel good to your body and regretted them later?

Day 77

For where your treasure is, there will your heart be also.
— Matthew 6:21

Where do you spend most of your money? On your family? On your hobbies? On your house? On vacations? On eating out at nice restaurants? Where would you continue to spend your money if your income was cut in half?

Day 78

A heart filled with love is like a phoenix that no cage can imprison. — Rumi

Have you ever crashed and burned at something in your life? Were you able to find a way to put yourself back together again? Were you able to rise up and be stronger because of the lessons you learned? Have you ever had a financial crisis?

Day 79

I can heal a broken heart with a smile. — Rumi

Do you know someone who has a smile that always makes you feel good when you see it? Do you smile at other people when you first meet them? What is the price for receiving a kind smile? Have you tried to heal someone's broken heart with your money instead of your attention/smile?

Day 80

The most expensive things we own are the things we never use. Do you have things that you bought and then you never used them? Why didn't you use them? What are the things you use everyday? Your cell phone? Your computer? If you average the cost of these things together, the price per use becomes very affordable.

Day 81

Look at the birds of the air; they do not sow or reap or store away in barns and yet your heavenly Father feeds them. — Matt. 6:26

Have you ever worried about having enough money to pay for food? Have you worried about running out of money? Isn't it amazing how the birds never worry or question that there will be food for them to eat?

Day 82

Behold how good and how pleasant it is for brethren to dwell together in unity.
— Psalm 133:1

Do you have unity in your home? In your family? In your neighborhood? If you do not live with unity around you, what interferes with the unity? Do differences of opinion separate you from others?

Day 83

Thou wilt keep him in perfect peace whose mind is stayed on thee. — Isaiah 26:3. These are meditation instructions from thousands of years ago. Focusing your thoughts on one or two words from this verse will help quiet your mind. The words I like are "perfect peace". Which words from this verse do you like?

Day 84

I will trust and not be afraid. — Isaiah 12:2

Do you trust in your own resources/abilities more than you trust in a Power greater than yourself? Are you able to trust and not be afraid in all circumstances? Are you able to trust and not be afraid about your financial choices? Are you able to trust and not be afraid of the choices of others?

Day 85

Let us not be satisfied with just giving money. Money is not enough, for money one can get. — Mother Teresa

Have you ever given money to make up for not spending time with someone? Or to make up for not donating volunteer time so you gave a nice donation of money instead? Do you agree that some people are so poor all they really have is money?

Day 86

We do more harm than good to young healthy people when we give them things. — Mother Teresa

Do you prefer to have someone's undivided attention instead of a material thing from them? Do you give material things to your children or other people's children instead of spending time with them?

Day 87

Happy is he who does not condemn himself. — Romans 14:22

Do you criticize yourself when you make a mistake? Or do you condemn yourself because "you should have known better"? Have you criticized or condemned yourself for making a financial mistake? Can you accept that you did the best you could at the time?

Day 88

Why spend money on what is not bread, and your labor on what does not satisfy? — Isaiah 55:2. Have you ever spent a lot of time on something only to find out later that it did not get you the results you expected? Do you spend your money on what is not "bread" (nourishing) for you? How did you feel after this happened?

Day 89

Praise the Lord your God, who has delighted in you. — 1 Kings 10:8

What do you delight in? Do you have someone in your life who delights in you and spending time with you? If you have people in your life that delight you, do you let them know how much you enjoy their company and having them as a part of your life?

Day 90

Before God we are all poor; we are all handicapped in one way or another.
— Mother Teresa. Do you know anyone who is handicapped? Do you treat them with kindness because you know they struggle with being handicapped? Do you know anyone who is emotionally or financially handicapped?

Day 91

I always say I am a little pencil in God's hands. He does the writing. — Mother Teresa — Do you ever think of God writing a message to the world through you? What is the message that God wants to send to the world through you? What do you want the message to be that gets delivered to the world through you?

Day 92

When I am afraid, I will trust in you.— Psalm 56:3

What do you do when you are afraid? What/Who do you trust when you are afraid? Do you trust that you can survive whatever is scaring you? Are you afraid of running out of money? Are you afraid of not having enough money when you retire?

Day 93

A happy heart makes the face cheerful. — Proverbs 15:13. Do you know people that you think of as being cheerful most of the time? What makes them so cheerful/happy? Are they people who have a lot of money? Are they people who do not have any big life problems? What is one thing you can do today to make your heart happier?

Day 94
Praise the beauty —
2 Chronicles 20:21 What is beautiful to you? A sunset and the beautiful colors in the sky? Pretty flowers growing naturally or in an arrangement? A newborn baby sleeping? Do you pay attention to the beauty around you as you go throughout your day? Can you make a list of the beauty in your life today?

Day 95

We consider blessed those who have persevered. — James 5:11. Have you ever had a situation or circumstance that went on and on and felt like it would never be over or resolved? Do you have anything going on in your life right now that you would like to be resolved faster than it is happening?

Day 96

Riches can suffocate if they are not used in the right way, whether they are spiritual riches or material.
— Mother Teresa

Do you know someone who you consider "rich" materially? Are they a happy person? Or are they really preoccupied with all of their "things" and taking care of their money/property?

Day 97

God gives us everything freely; we must also give what we have, give ourselves. Whatever you give, make sure you have it to give. — Mother Teresa

Have you ever helped someone to the point that you were physically exhausted afterwards? Have you ever helped someone financially and given away too much and hurt your budget?

Day 98

God — being connected to a Universe that celebrates life.
— Louis Schwartzberg

What is your definition of God? Do you believe in a Universe that is designed to celebrate life? Have you ever noticed that leaves blowing in the wind look like hand clapping? What is something worth celebrating in your life today?

Day 99

He is not the God of the dead, but the God of the living. — Mark 12:27

Do you ever think of God as being the source of life and death? Do you know people who are like the "walking dead"? Do you know people who are vibrant and full of life (no matter how old they are)? Which people do you prefer to spend time with?

Day 100

Array thyself with glory and beauty. — Job 40:10

What would it mean to you to array (dress) yourself with glory and beauty? Do you think it is selfish to dress yourself with beauty everyday? Do you think it is a gift to other people if you are dressed with beauty everyday? Do you enjoy seeing people who are dressed with beauty?

Day 101

God breathed the breath of life into his nostrils. — Genesis 2:7. Our lives begin when we take our first breath as babies and when we die, people say that we "took our last breath". No one can live without their breath. Do you pay attention to your breathing? Can you spend some time today paying attention to your breathing?

Day 102

All things share the same breath — the beast, the tree, the man. The air shares its spirit with all the life it supports — Chief Seattle

Do you ever think about how we all share the same air — back and forth? Do you ever think about how the air around us connects every human being on the planet? Are you grateful for your breath?

Day 103

Now that you know these things, you will be blessed if you do them. — John 13:17

Have you ever learned something that you consider a real blessing in your life? Are prayer and meditation a blessing in your life? What is something you can do today that will be a blessing for someone else or yourself?

Day 104

...for I have learned to be content whatever the circumstances — Philippians 4:11. Are you content and satisfied with all of the circumstances in your life? Are you able to accept all of the circumstances in your life even though you might not like all of them? Which/what circumstances would you like to change if you could?

Day 105

Do not be deceived. Evil company corrupts good habits. 1 Cor. 15:33. Do you know anyone who acts completely different when they are around certain people? Do you behave differently when you get around certain groups of people? Do the other people influence how you choose to spend your money?

Day 106

Command those who are rich in this present age not to trust in uncertain riches. — 1 Timothy 6:17. Do you know anyone who thinks their money can solve any problem that happens to them? Do you know anyone who trusted in their money more than they trusted in God? What are the things in your life money cannot buy?

Day 107

What do you have that you did not receive? — 1 Cor. 4:7. Everything we have came from somewhere — the store, as a gift, from someone we know, etc. Take a minute and think of all of the "things" (including relationships and abilities) and where they came from? What is your favorite thing and where did it come from?

Day 108

You will show me the path that leads to life; your presence fills me with joy.
— Psalm 16:11. Do you know anyone whose presence fills you with joy? Do you know anyone who makes you feel more alive and vital when you spend time with them? What are "life-giving" choices for you in your daily life?

Positive Words and Traits

Part of the effects of living with or around addiction is to be very negative in your speech and your thoughts — especially towards yourself. This is a list of positive words for every letter of the alphabet except for the letter "X" to help you start

developing a positive vocabulary for describing and talking about and to yourself.

Aloha
Admirable
Awesome
Attentive
Alive
Adorable
Alert

Assertive
Accountable
Awake
Amazing
Accepting
Attractive
Articulate
Artistic
Authentic
Appropriate
Approachable
Appreciative
Affectionate

Active

Able

Agreeable

Accomplished

Abundant

All right

Aware

Am

Beloved

Beautiful

Bright

Brave

Brilliant
Best
Becoming
Bold
Bountiful
Balanced
Benevolent
Beaming
Blessed
Better

Cute
Calm

Curious
Celebrate
Courageous
Contagious
Charming
Clever
Cheerful
Capable
Careful
Cautious
Complex
Connected
Consistent

Comical
Comforting
Creative
Caring
Confident
Competent
Civilized
Complete
Child of God
Considerate
Compassionate
Contributing
Collaborative

Conscientious
Coachable

Dandy
a Dancer
Dynamite
Delightful
Dedicated
Devoted
Dear
Dynamic
Determined
Daring

Darling
Dutiful
Delicious
Deserving
Discerning
Durable
Divine
Dreamer
Diligent
Dainty
Desirable
Dependable

Eminent
Exalted
Eternal
Evolving
Enough
Emotional
Endearing
Employable
Even-tempered
Energetic
Excellent
Ecstasy
Euphoric

Expressive
Engaging
Exquisite
Exemplary
Exciting
Exceptional
Earnest
Enterprising
Enchanting
Enjoyable
Endurance
Encouraging
Efficient

Entertaining
Enthusiastic
Effective
Empathetic
Experienced
Empowered
Effervescent
Extraordinary
Exuberant
Enthralling

Flawless
Fun/funny

Fantastic
Fabulous
Friendly
Fearless
Faithful
Fanciful
Fashionable
Fast
Flexible
Famous
Fit
Fulfilled
Focused

Frugal
Free
Fortuitous
Fresh
so Fine
Fascinating
First Class

Glowing
Glorious
Grateful
Glamorous
Great

Gracious
Giving
Grace-filled
Generous
Gifted
Gorgeous
Genuine
Girly
Gregarious
Gentle
Grounded

Helpful

Honest
Hardworking
Heroic
Healthy
Happy
"Hot"
Humorous
Healer
Honorable
Hope/hopeful
Harmonizing
Handsome
Hilarious

Helper
Humble
Holy
Healthy

Informed
Impressive
Intelligent
Introspective
Interesting
Intuitive
Inventive
Intriguing

Insightful
Industrious
Illuminating
Infinite
Invincible
Independent
Indispensable
Impeccable
Influential
Integrity
Inspirational
Invigorating
Irresistible

Incredible
Inspiring
Important
Insightful
Intriguing
Improving

Jovial
Judicious
Jubilant
Jolly
Joking
Just

Kind
Knowledgeable
Knack-ful
Kindred
Kooky
Kazowie
Kissable

Lucky
Loving
Loyal
Likable

Laughing
Life-giving
Limitless
Lively
Lovable
Lighthearted
Luscious
Lustrous
Lovable
Learned
Loyal
Listener
Loved

Learning every day
Life
Light

Mighty
Motivated
Ministering
Mature
Magnificent
Magnanimous
Mindful
Merciful
Merry

Motherly
Melodious
Meticulous
Magical
Memorable
Me
Matter
Musical
Miraculous
Masterful
Monumental
Marvelous
Masterpiece

Needed
Nice
Neat
Noticeable
Nurturing
Noble
Natural
Nourishing
Nifty
New
Neighborly
Necessary

Outstanding
Organized
Open
Open-minded
Optimistic
One of a kind
Original
Outgoing
Opulent
Observant
Okay

Perfect
Polite
Passionate
Potential
Popular
Progressive
Positive
Patient
Productive
Pretty
Peaceful
Pleasant
Precious

Perceptive
Protective
Perseverant
Present
Polished
Praiseworthy
Practical
Punctual
Powerful
Protective
Principled
a Phoenix
Playful

Pure potential
Persistent
Peachy keen
Proper

Quiet
Quality
Questioning
Quirky
Quick
Quaint

Responsible

Real
Reflective
Realistic
Reasonable
Resourceful
Ravishing
Right
Radiant
Relevant
Reassuring
Relaxed
Romantic
Respected

Restored
Reliable
Rare
Remarkable
Rosy
Rested

Superb
Stunning
Significant
Spectacular
Sweet
Sincere

Sympathetic
Smart
Sensational
Super
Splendid
Sensitive
Social
Satisfied
Soothing
Spiritual
Stable
Special delivery
Strong

Smiley
Saintly
Selective
Sunny
Stylish
Successful
Serene
Simple
Smashing
Sleek
Swift
Safe
Silly

Studious
Secure
Sharing
Scientific
Serenity
Special
Supporting/supportive
Super star
Swell
Superlicious
Scintillating
Scrumptious

Talented
Transformational
Trustworthy
Tremendous
Terrific
Truthful
Thoughtful
Thankful
Tough
Teachable
Timeless
Tenacious
Team player

Tender
Tried and true
Thorough
Tolerant
Thrifty
Touching
Trim
Titillating

Universal
Unique
Understanding
Unbelievable

Uplifting
Unity
Useful
Unparalleled
Unbounded

Vivacious
Vital
Vibrant
Valuable
Victorious
Vulnerable

Well
Wonderful
Willing
Wise
Whimsical
Winning
Worthy
Watchful
Wholesome
Winner
Wow
Witty
Washed

Whole
Warm
Worthwhile
Wisdom
Wanted
a Work of Art
Woohoo

Youthful
Young at heart
Yummy
Yowza
Yes

Yielding
Yahoo

Zowie
Zealous
Zestful

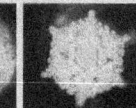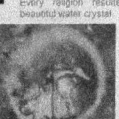

Masuru Emoto — Emoto Peace Project
Masuru Emoto — 1943 - 2014

www.ingramcontent.com/pod-product-compliance
Lightning Source LLC
Chambersburg PA
CBHW061949070426
42450CB00007BA/1098